A Heart Transformed

Workings of the Great Physician

Anna Marie Valentine

Made with ❤ on the BookLeaf Publishing Platform
www.bookleafpub.in
www.bookleafpub.com

Dedication

This book of poetry is dedicated to any person who believes that their story is not over. That old patterns and generational curses are merely stepping stones to the purification of your heart. You, my friend, are a masterpiece. Every part of your heart, mind and soul were crafted by the Creator who designed you with attention to detail, specific gifts and a remarkable calling.

To my husband, Matthew. Your wit, humor, and encouragement keep me light and inspired. To Lainey. You will never believe the amount of fun, joy, love and creativity you have taught me. To my mom. No one compares to your love, your heart, and your model for my life. To my dad. Thank you for believing in me and encouraging me to KNOW that I can achieve whatever dream is placed on my heart.

Lastly, to Jesus. My life would not be possible without your grace, your compassion and your design. Thank you for your favor in allowing me to author this book of poetry. May the words inspire, glorify, and honor you.

Preface

Cultivating a life of faith and a relationship with Jesus is a gift for everyone. It is not a free handout to live by our ego's desires but to surrender to the idea that we do not know what we are doing.

This book draws upon my early experiences with Christianity. I was born into an upper-middle-class family and was privileged to attend a private Christian school. Though I can look back and appreciate the doctrine being presented, my young heart could not make sense of the idea that I was in charge of my faith. Jesus was presented as a tangible figure to praise and worship without a deeper understanding of what it was like to be genuinely in a relationship with Him. Religion felt fictitious and dismissive to me as an adolescent. I hope these poems give you a depiction of my heart surgery. Through relationships, I have come to know my creator. Religion and church are a gift, but without the spirit of the Lord, I do not know how I would have made it. I owe him my life, and I hope these pages instill hope within you that you have been given the same gift. You are special. You were created for a purpose. You matter. You are loved. You ARE love. In Jesus name,

Anna Marie Valentine

Acknowledgements

I want to thank my Lord Jesus for finding me in all of my broken places and for your continued grace day in and day out. Thank you to my husband, Matthew, for always encouraging me to pursue my creativity and dreams. Thank you to Lainey for your fun-loving spirit.

Thank you to my family at March Christian Counseling. Working alongside believers has been a necessary dream come true. Shannon, thank you for your brave leadership. Madeline and Stephen, thank you for portraying the hands and feet of Jesus. Tracey and Ebony, thank you for your support and friendship. Allen, thank you for your kindness and humor. Lynley, thank you for your constant check-ins and support. Jessie, thank you for your realness. Marni, thank you for just being the most extraordinary woman alive. Rebecca, thank you for being so encouraging, calm, and loving. Julie, thank you for your dear friendship.

Thank you to every one of my clients. You exhibit resilience, perseverance, and grit day in and day out. You will never understand how much you inspire me to keep moving forward.

Thank you to my friends Grace Ardila, Kyrstin Korbe, Emily Fadool, Vicky Castain, Elena Rogers, Carolina Jaime, Kaycee Sullivan, Bobbi Jayne Gordon, Sunni Walton, Mattie Welborn, Tammy Kolbo, L.C. Dawson, Halle-Brook Barnard, Sara Richardson, Haley Slaton, Megan Valentine, and Melissa Booth. Each of you has truly inspired and uplifted me in this season of life.

Thank you to my brother, Donald, my dad, and my momma. Thank you to Monica and Robert Valentine for welcoming me with open arms. And, of course, I thank Wilson and Cooper for showing me love, innocence, and gentleness.

Cover art by: Ms. Lainey Valentine

1. In the Beginning...

As a child, we begin,
this journey toward becoming.
No concept of sin.
No loss or shortcomings.

We wonder and play.
We laugh and we cry.
Pretend and ballet,
always, new things to try.

As we grow older,
we learn "right from wrong".
We cry on the shoulders
of friends, dad, and mom.

We learn to survive.
The magic subsides.
Each day, we strive,
rules and emotions as guides.

Yet we wonder inside
what's just beyond our view.
We begin to decide
what is good and what is true.

2. Kid Stuff

I still remember how
my school smelled like glue.
Our lunches were the same.
Quizzes out of the blue.

Classrooms full of order.
The same chapel songs,
Music class with the recorder,
Walking in lines to move us along.

I was introduced to God.
But nothing felt real.
He seemed like a fraud.
A man that could heal?

Being a kid means
no dream is too grand.
The world is your canvas.
The brush in your hand.

But something like faith.
We were expected to believe.
We did not express doubt.
We were taught to receive.

I thought something was wrong.
My belief was not like theirs.
I worshipped and sang songs
but felt alone in my prayers.

It was not until later
that I pursued Him myself.
As almighty Creator.
Desperate for health.

It would be a long journey,
To change and transform.
But doubt was important,
so there could be reform.

3. Fragments of Youth

Seventh grade was a storm
I could not out run.
Searching for self,
yet finding no one.

Personalities to try
and see what might fit.
An identity of pieces,
we build bit by bit.

Our hearts can surely break.
As self-awareness begins.
So much is at stake,
in a race no one wins.

The fun of yesterday.
Is replaced by the fear.
Joy and laughter fades,
as growing up draws near.

The same depiction of God.
Consumes our daily schedule.
But hearts grow restless, seeking
A truth that's more than ritual.

Questions linger quietly,
About the truth of this story.
Where could I find Him?
Where was His glory?

Yet, I have to hold fast.
To a season that hurt.
The pain would not last,
and later taught me my worth.

4. Paper Hearts and Heavy Minds

We leave our home to become great,
We venture out with a false, clean slate.
We fold our hearts like paper cranes,
Fragile art from joy and pains.

We live from ego, pride, and shame.
We hurt and blunder; life's a game.
But deep within, Lord Jesus whispers
This is not the way; please remember my name.

We go on chasing with a lack of humility.
Rejection is a sting we do not accept willingly.
We chase personal endeavors to prove our success.
Yet, inside, we feel empty; our heart is a mess.

With heavy minds and hopeful hands,
We try to sketch our lives with no reprimand.
But paper hearts can tear with ease,
In winds of doubt, they bend and freeze.

Though we often wear a disguise,
we have weary hearts and tired eyes.
Holding onto hope, our life unwinds
with paper hearts and heavy minds.

5. The Mountain Climb

In our stories, there comes a time
to change our course and pursue a climb.
We come upon a mountain that reaches the skies
to move up or around, many choices arise.

Confident or not, we decide on a fate.
We must plunge forward or risk something great.
We believe this is it; the time to prevail
yet without our Lord Jesus, we are likely to fail.

We face many twists to climb up the ladder,
Minds always racing, our hearts growing sadder.
As we persist, suffer turmoil and strain,
We push through the struggle, embracing the pain.

We search for our purpose.
Life feels like a circus.
We do the right things.
We're spreading our wings.

We learn to pay bills.
Our nights full of thrills.
We think that we've got it
using our will and our grit.

But at some point it feels
like we've been spinning our wheels.
We are stopped in our tracks
as we acknowledge the cracks.

We knew this day would arrive
when we could no longer strive.
We're hit with the fact,
We cannot keep up the act.

We need a Physician,
who can meet us in this position.
To restore our sense of life,
to remove the pain and strife.

We look to the sky,
we laugh and we cry.
If there is someone above,
please.. show me some love.

This is the moment,
we choose our atonement.

We surrender our heart,
Could it be that now life can start?

6. Waffling Winds

It starts with a choice,
to listen for His voice.
We continue to operate,
Many thoughts to regenerate.

We start with a passion
for grace and compassion.
Hearing nothing but silence.
Where is His reliance?

We're supposed to feel Him,
yet this light feels so dim.
Our prayers are ignored,
We do not feel restored.

The devotion drifts away.
Our days on replay.
We go through the motions,
ignoring our emotions.

We gave it a shot.
played church and whatnot.
We feel so alone,
the pain cuts to the bone.

Out of the blue,
we see something new.
What was once a dark dream
doesn't feel so extreme.

Could this be hope?
At the end of our rope.
We consider letting go.
Yet, the Father whispers, "no".

In the smallest of ways,
He reveals that he stays.
We cling to the desire
that He will take us higher.

7. Haunted by Maybe

The journey to freedom
begins with a wisdom.
To acknowledge the past
to find peace at last.

We cannot go forward
unless we move toward
the truth of our story
to reveal a new glory.

We avoid being known.
Stay afraid and alone.
Yet, there is always a call
to break down the wall.

To allow a new sight
to bring shame to the light.
It's no easy decision.
Truth causes collision.

Regrets carry weight.
Block our free fate.
We must reveal from our heart
before the Lord's work can start.

So maybe it's true
we could have a new view
of our past circumstances
had we not taken chances.

But the Lord allows us to break
to know what's at stake.
We must choose surrender,
Until He becomes our defender.

8. Open Heart Surgery

He begins a long process,
when we give Him the access.
To strip away the YOU
to make someone new.

We begin to transform
within this reform.
What used to berate
does not agitate.

We start to see others
as sisters and brothers.
The peace that we feel,
just does not seem real.

It starts to make sense.
We're less on defense.
We see people with pain.
With nothing to gain.

Could it have been all along?
He's been writing our song.
Yet we played with no strings.
Separated from love that He brings.

It's a slow rewiring.
The ideas begin firing.
Some days filled with passion.
And a deep sense of compassion.

The truth of our being.
We weren't fully seeing.
We've opened our heart,
to allow God to start.

He's gentle and kind.
We're happy to find
His love never ends,
Even when our thoughts bend.

This moment in time
has been quite a climb.
To lay down our burdens,
our mind become gardens.

He sows inner seeds.
To supply all our needs.

This open heart surgery.
A sanctifying emergency.

9. Shame Stopper

We get stuck in our mind.
On fast forward or rewind.
We look to the past.
And try to forecast.

Like a loop on repeat.
We remember defeat.
The future looks bleak.
Yet peace, we still seek.

We question our motives.
Ask for perspectives.
Using counselors and friends,
to make our amends.

The truth of the matter
is that we must calm the clatter.
Release what has been–
before true life can begin.

Yet shame is a bear
we're nervous to share.
We grip on so tight
rather than look at the light.

We get trapped in our storms.
Distorted narratives form.
We sink in the shame.
We can't give it a name.

One day we realize,
as we open our eyes.
We're living in a reality
of a dark, skewed mentality.

That is when life begins.
We shed our past sins.
We breathe the crisp air.
We become more aware.

Our life is right now.
If we will only allow.
Our minds to be here.
The Lord becomes near.

10. The Potter with Clay

Our bodies represent
what we cannot prevent.
A darkness shines through
in the things that we do.

Jesus lovingly reveals
all the places he heals.
Our hearts are so cold,
yet he begins to mold.

Our souls just like clay
as He shows us the way.
To live a new life
Less worry and strife.

Though we feel the free gift
our thoughts start to shift.
We realize our role
rooted down in our soul.

He serves as the potter.
He whispers, "Sweet daughter.."
He holds us so tight.
We resist with our might.

We know deep inside
in His truth we abide.
We commit to the change
of our minds to re-arrange.

Like a potter with clay,
we read and we pray.
We know our truth hope
is at the end of our rope.

11. I AM FINE

I once had a supervisor
who served as my visualizer.
Each day he would ask
if I felt up to the task.

Inside I was dying.
I spent my nights crying.
I worked in a prison
this was my decision.

He would ask with a smile
if I would spend a while
addressing the pain
that was consuming my brain.

"How are you?" he'd ask.
I would put on the mask.
"Today, I am fine."
Yet, no light would shine.

Danny taught me how fine
just did not align
with the truth my face.
He said to "hold space".

This internship taught me
the key to be free.
To acknowledge our feelings.
which leads to the healings.

The Lord is my guide.
I lay down my pride.
These emotions he gave me.
Will help me to see.

I need Him to lead.
Before He plants the seed.
To move into calling.
Without stumbling or crawling.

12. The Joy of Pain

What a true paradox
to realize the blocks
we encounter mentally
would humble us gently.

The more that we see
our pain is the key
to teach us what we do not know
so we can move and grow.

I would know nothing without
all the fear and the doubt.
What is He doing?
Girl, he is renewing.

He's giving you sight.
Your heart is a light.
He designed you with love
to share His world above.

Your pain is what made you.
Your hurt is what's true.
Your story is the vehicle
to lead others to their miracle.

Suffering is not the end.
You don't have to pretend.
He gives you a new heart.
This is just the start.

He will use your whole story.
To reveal His true glory.
Keep your eyes up above
on His unfailing love.

The joy of pain gives
the hope that He lives.
Without all the hardship,
you would not be equipped.

13. Breathe and Believe

You will reach a moment
when you face the opponent.
He may be hard to notice,
but tune in and focus.

He is sneaky and sly;
he will whisper a lie.
That maybe you should question:
"Is there really a redemption?"

He reminds you of loss,
we question the cross.
He tempts you to lie
to give up and not try.

We feel weak and tired,
we assume that is how we are wired.
The enemy is doing works,
behind us he lurks.

If we notice the pattern,
we begin to discern.
What comes from the Lord,
and what lies we can't afford.

But take a step back.
He is on the attack.
Guard your heart and mind.
You are no longer blind.

Breathe and surrender.
So gentle and tender.
Your mind is a battle.
The enemy wants to rattle.

Jesus is on your team.
Even though it may seem
that the world is crashing down.
But He wears the crown.

14. Again and again...

We start a new day
Intent on the way
to spend time with Jesus
in strength and in weakness.

Yet we do realize-
again, believing the lies.
We repent and give up.
Please refill our cup.

We restart our mind
attempt to be kind.
Again we get triggered.
Has our faith withered?

I want to be new.
To have a clear view
of the life I was promised
if I am just being honest.

I have followed and cried.
I have tried, and I've tried, and I've tried...
Yet I am left feeling hopeless.
The pain feels so endless.

But no matter the cost,
I will seek what is lost.
The Lord will restore.
If I do not ignore.

Know that it's typical
to not always feel biblical.
We're just a mere person.
That much is certain.

15. Cumulative Progress

Each small decision
creates a new vision.
Each step that we take
begins to create.

A new way of living
to continue giving
our heart to the world
so humanity can be restored.

Jesus shows us the way
as we start a new day.
Each moment, a choice.
To listen for His voice.

In sleeping and wake.
We can't take a break.
When we try on our own
Our cover is blown.

But in the blink of an eye.
We continue to try
to display the light
through our grit and our fight.

Sometimes it's okay
to pray for a way
to endure the hard years
through suffering and fears.

We cling to the hope
that we truly can cope.
And life has a reason,
we had to face each season.

So take the next step.
He has started to prep
the fruit of your labor.
Thank God for our Savior.

16. Do you see it?

Could it really be?
Is that...me?
Doing things different.
No longer as ignorant.

I see people in a way
that begs me to pray
for the comfort of their heart.
We are all set apart.

Life is not always just.
Love is a must.
We need one another.
To help us uncover

the weight of our minds.
That keeps us shackled in binds.
When we are able to share.
We see that others care.

Their love is a gift.
Our minds can also shift.
To the glory that abounds.
To love that is all around.

This life is a mystery.
But in the right company.
We feel seen and known.
It's like coming home.

To a new perspective.
Reality is subjective.
But we can now clearly see.
We were always meant to be.

Thank you, dear Jesus.
For all of the sweetness.
That comes from your sheep.
Their love runneth deep.

17. Hi Jesus, it's Me...

Hello up there.
There's a lot I would like to share.
You've known me forever.
I have changed however.

You prewrote my story.
To display your glory.
I wandered so lost.
No matter the cost.

At the end of my rope.
I was left with no hope.
I looked to the sky.
To face the most high.

I took a deep breath.
So close to my death.
You made me brand new.
So good, and so true.

My heart is like clay.
Each and every day.
You prompt me to move.
My sin, you remove.

You are nothing but love.
When we look up above.
You have always been there.
With deep reverence and care.

You are humble and kind.
Our memories rewind.
But you hold us right here.
So close, and so near.

So thank you for waiting.
I know you were creating
a fresh, new perspective.
That has been your objective.

I promise to honor
the truth of my Father
who wants me to win
this battle with sin.

It makes so much sense
why life was intense.

My soul needed comfort.
To mend up the hurt.

I am now a new person.
A shiny new version.
To reflect your heart.
Each day, a new start.

18. Well done, my love.

One day, I will lie down.
In a soft, cozy gown.
It will serve as an ending.
To start a new beginning.

Again, I will look high.
to see You in the sky.
I will see your pure face.
I will feel your embrace.

Well done, my sweet love.
You will speak from above.
A life whole of service.
To maintain my promise.

I gave you my life.
I served as a wife.
I served as a friend.
Until the very end.

It was not always perfect.
I know you could detect.
Yet I kept coming back
to stay on Your track.

You blessed me immensely.
I do not say that lightly.
I hope I made you proud
of my life you endowed.

I am afraid, and I am sure.
The next step is a pure
depiction of You.
I know that is true.

But it still feels unclear.
I feel hope AND fear.
Of the next chapter to come.
Yet you whisper, "well done".

I rest now embracing
this path we've been chasing.
A life without pain,
I am surely to gain.

It is okay not to know
where I will go.

You transformed my heart.
It is time to depart.

Thank you for the chance
to live life as a dance.
What a beautiful ride.
You served as my guide.

Take care of my children.
They need Jesus, for certain.
Show them the way.
To be still and pray.

I am at peace
Nothing to release.
Comfort them to know.
It was time for me to grow.